ROBIN HOOD

by

Michael Macfarlane

Cornelsen

Robin Hood
Michael Macfarlane

Verlagsredaktion
Sandhya Gupta

Umschlaggestaltung
Heike Börner, Berlin

Titelbilder
Mary Evans Picture Library / Alamy
Corel Library

Illustration
Roy Schofield

Technische Umsetzung
Christian Seifert

www.cornelsen.de

1. Auflage, 3. Druck 2019

Alle Drucke dieser Auflage sind inhaltlich unverändert und können im Unterricht nebeneinander verwendet werden.

Druck und Bindung: Livonia Print, Riga

ISBN 978-3-464-37167-1

PEFC
PEFC/12-31-006

PEFC zertifiziert
Dieses Produkt stammt aus nachhaltig bewirtschafteten Wäldern und kontrollierten Quellen.

www.pefc.de

CONTENTS

PART 1

THE START OF THE ROBIN HOOD STORIES

1 Dark times in England

In 1066, an army crossed the sea to England. The English army fought these Normans hard, but the Normans won. The English king, Harold, died that day and the man who led the Normans – William – became the next king of England.

For the English, people who came from Germany 500 years before, this was a terrible time. The Normans took their land and became their new lords all over the country. They were very different people, and they spoke French, not the German-English language of the people of England. They brought lots of clever new ideas, but they were also often cruel to the ordinary people of England.

This went on for over 100 years, but things started to get better when Richard 'the Lion Heart' became king in 1189. He was Norman, but the ordinary people loved this brave and popular soldier-king. At last the English started to hate the Normans less.

But this was the time when Christian armies from Europe went to 'the Holy Land' and fought to take it from the Muslims. Sadly for England, King Richard led one of these armies to the Holy Land and was away from home for five years. Richard's brother, John, then took control of the country, and he was very different. He was cruel, and even the cruellest lords were afraid of him.

For ordinary people, these years were difficult and dangerous. And this was when the stories and songs about Robin Hood began – a thief who took from the rich and gave to the poor. They also said that he loved King Richard and hated evil Prince John. Soon, Robin Hood was the hero of the poor, unhappy people of England.

Was Robin Hood a real person? Nobody really knows. Perhaps he was more than one person. Most stories say that he lived in Sherwood Forest near Nottingham, but some say that he lived in other places. Perhaps he moved from place to place.

We will never know the true facts about 'the prince of thieves' who was 'loved by the poor, feared by the rich'. But whatever those facts were, the stories of Robin Hood are still famous and popular today, nearly 1,000 years later.

2 Is Robin Hood real?

In the great, dark hall of Nottingham Castle a fire burned brightly at one end. A hundred men were laughing, talking, shouting, eating and drinking.

At the Sheriff's table a man with a thin, cold face and cold, black eyes turned to a fat, older man. 'Sheriff,' he said, 'tell me about this outlaw, Robin Hood, who lives in Sherwood Forest. Even far away in London people talk about him. They say he takes from the rich and gives to the poor. And this is bad, isn't it?'

The Sheriff of Nottingham laughed loudly and said to his guest, Prince John, 'Sir, you mustn't believe these stories. Yes, there are a few thieves in the forest, but there's nothing to worry about. Really.'

'But *is* there a real Robin Hood?'

'They're just stupid stories for children. Believe me.'

Just then, a knight in armour entered the hall. There was something wrong. He seemed tired as he moved slowly towards the Sheriff's table. His face was dirty and covered with blood. It was the Sheriff's cousin, cruel Sir Guy of Gisborne. The hall became very quiet.

'Well, cousin Guy, have you brought me more gold from the people today? Prince John here needs more gold.'

Sir Guy reached the table and – and nearly fell. 'We had gold, but ...'

'But what?' The Sheriff said quickly.

'We were attacked in the forest.'

'And?'

'They got the gold and killed five of my men.'

'Was it ...?'

Sir Guy closed his eyes and nodded slowly.

Prince John's cold eyes turned from Sir Guy to the Sheriff and back again. 'Just another stupid Robin Hood story, eh?' There was no answer. 'Well, what now, Sheriff?' He was angry.

The Sheriff hit the table angrily and said, 'Ride with me tomorrow. I'll get you gold. And I'll show you who controls Sherwood!'

'But who is this Robin Hood? Can you show me that?'

3 An evil morning at the mill

Early next day, the Sheriff rode out with Prince John, Sir Guy and some soldiers. They rode through the town gate, past the cattle market, and they took the road towards Sherwood Forest.

At the market, two men were finishing some business. Twenty-five gold coins changed hands – one for each of the fat, black cows behind them. One man turned away and looked at his new animals more carefully. The other, a man with a scar across his face, put 20 coins into a red bag. The others he quietly put in his pocket. 'My good, simple-minded master needn't know about these. Anyway, he just gives his money to the poor or the sick. Stupid! I can use the money much better.'

He looked up as the Sheriff and the others rode past. 'Hmm ... he's with Prince John – and with soldiers. Where are they going?' He decided to follow. 'Who knows?' he thought. 'Perhaps I can find myself a more sensible master.' He waited, then got on his horse and followed.

***

The Sheriff was laughing and joking, but Prince John's thin mouth hardly smiled. The Sheriff was in fact very nervous. He needed gold, and he had to show that he, not Robin Hood, controlled Sherwood.

For these things, he needed Sir Guy's help, and Sir Guy led the way. They passed through a small, poor village. Frightened mothers pushed thin, dirty children into the little huts and shut their doors. In the fields, men stood up from their hard work and watched the rich men – men that they hated.

Sir Guy knew that there was no gold there. Everything that the village people had was already all in Nottingham Castle.

But he had a different idea, and he pointed the way ahead. They rode on towards the forest.

Soon afterwards, another man rode past the village. A man with a scar.

***

Sir Guy led the group off the Sherwood road and down a cart track. It took them to a river and a mill with trees around it. A cart with some large bags of flour was standing outside, and wood smoke was coming from the roof of the mill. 'Good,' Sir Guy thought. 'Much the Miller is at home.' As a miller, Much knew all the farmers and everything about Sherwood. 'If anyone knows about Robin Hood, Much the Miller does.'

An older man, about 50 but strong, came to the door with a bag of flour on his back. He threw the bag onto the cart, and then turned to Sir Guy. He said nothing. They were not friends.

'Good morning,' said his visitor. 'You're a busy man, and a busy man is a rich man. So why haven't you paid your taxes?'

'I have, and you know it. Your men have taken everything.'

'I mean special taxes for millers who know about Robin Hood. Of course, if you tell me where he is, perhaps …'

'I can't tell you anything about Robin Hood,' Much said. He looked Sir Guy straight in the eye.

'Can't? Or do you mean 'won't'?

'Go back to Nottingham, and leave us Sherwood people alone.'

'A stupid answer, Much, so it's time for a lesson.' Sir Guy turned to his men. 'Burn the mill!' he shouted. And to Much he said, 'I think we'll burn you, too.' He shouted again: 'Get him!' Some of the soldiers grabbed Much. Others got ready to burn the mill.

'Wait,' shouted Sir Guy to his men. 'One more time, old man. Who and where is Robin Hood?'

'Well, if you kill me, you'll never find out,' Much answered.

'But if I kill you, perhaps other people around here will talk.'

***

Just then, a boy, about 15 years old, appeared from between the trees. 'What's happening, Father?' he called.

Sir Guy said to his men, 'Get the boy. If the old man won't talk to save himself, perhaps he'll talk to save his son.'

'Run and save your life, boy!' the old man shouted. 'Run!'

The boy stared, horrified. Three soldiers started towards him.

Suddenly, the old man pulled himself away from the Sheriff's men, grabbed a sword from one soldier, swung it at another and shouted again, 'Run! Save yourself!'

The boy finally turned and disappeared, the soldiers close behind. Meanwhile, old Much swung the sword again, shouted and ran towards Sir Guy, the Sheriff and Prince John. He knew he must die. Now he just wanted them to die, too. And he almost reached Prince John, the sword high above his head.

But at that second, an arrow flew past the Prince and hit the old man in the heart. With a terrible scream, Much fell to the ground and died.

4 What happened to Much the Miller's son

Prince John and the others turned and saw a man on the track. He had a long bow in his hand. It was the man with the scar.

'Thank you for saving my life,' Prince John said. 'Who are you?'

'My name is Worman, and I'm the servant of Robert Locksley, the Earl of Huntingdon.'

'Ah, the strange Earl Robert,' laughed Sir Guy. 'He never visits Nottingham and never meets the other lords. He's half-English and doesn't seem to like our Norman way of life.' Sir Guy did not like Earl Robert.

Prince John was interested. 'If he's not for us, perhaps he's against us,' he thought. He looked carefully at Worman. 'Is he against us?'

'He's for King Richard, your brother, sir.'

'King Richard! King Richard!' Prince John said angrily. 'My brother went away to the Holy Land and he's probably dead.

I'm going to be the King soon, and people like this Robert Locksley must learn that – or die.' He turned to the Sheriff. 'I think we should find out more about Locksley.'

Worman saw his chance. 'Sir,' he said, 'Earl Robert is my lord, it's true, but you're lord of all England, and so I should help you – and I can.'

'Go on.'

'Tomorrow night, there will be a feast at Locksley House for his marriage the next day to Lady Marian Fitzwalter.'

Sir Guy's eyes burned. This was why he hated Earl Robert. The beautiful Lady Marian wanted that half-English man, and not himself, Sir Guy of Gisborne.

Prince John nodded and turned back to Worman. 'What's your plan?'

'Locksley House will be open to everybody tomorrow night. So come in disguise. Say that you have come from the Holy Land and talk about King Richard. Then Earl Robert will talk openly with you.'

'A good idea, and you,' Prince John turned to the Sheriff, 'can come with me as another knight from the war.'

The Sheriff was not happy about this but decided he could not say no.

'And now,' said Sir Guy, 'let's burn the mill.' He was a man who really loved his work.

Later, he and the others laughed and joked as they rode away.

But Prince John was quiet. He had a strange feeling about Earl Robert.

***

Young Much knelt beside his poor, dead father. Behind him,

the fire was still burning, and he coughed in the black smoke as he cried over the body. Black soot fell over the two of them, father and son.

One of the people who came to help was a tall, strong-looking man in a forest green jacket who the local people called Will Scarlet. They knew little about him – only that he was Robin Hood's friend and servant. Will put his arm around the boy, and Much slowly began to tell his terrible story. 'And I did nothing to save my father,' he finally finished. 'I ran away like a frightened rabbit.'

'You're alive and that's the important thing,' Will answered. 'And your father did well to say nothing about Robin Hood.'

'But what now? They've killed my father, burned the mill, destroyed everything.' Much looked around, and he held his father's head in his arms.

'Come with me,' said Will. 'And start a new life with Robin Hood. We need strong, young men like you.'

'If I join Robin Hood and learn to fight, perhaps one day I'll be able to punish the evil people who've done all this – Sir Guy and the others.'

'But who killed your father?' Will wondered. 'This isn't the sort of arrow that the Sheriff's men use. It's the sort that we use in the forest.'

'I didn't see the man who killed my father,' said Much, 'but I'll find him. And when I do, I'll ...' He shook with anger.

'Sh, now, Much. This isn't the right time for that. We must bury your poor father now, and say goodbye to him properly.'

Before they buried him, Much asked for a minute alone with his father. He took the arrow from his father's body. He cleaned the blood from it, but left on it the black soot from the fire. 'With this black arrow,' he promised his father, 'I'll one day destroy the evil man who destroyed you.'

5 The feast at Locksley House

Late next day, two knights, one thin and young, the other older and heavier, arrived at Locksley House. Both wore rusty, old armour, and their faces were dark 'from the hot sun of the Holy Land,' the younger knight explained. 'That's where we've fought with the King for the last two years.'

Worman took the strangers into the hall and to the table of Earl Robert. There also sat Lady Marian and old Sir Patrick Fitzwalter, her father.

On the way, they passed tables of food and drink for 100 guests. Many of the people near Earl Robert's table were in forest green, and they looked like hard, outdoor men. Worman explained, 'They're foresters, and they're also Earl Robert's bodyguards. They go with him everywhere and their leader is William Scathlope. He's Earl Robert's favourite servant, and it's strange that he's not here this evening.'

The two knights sat down at Earl Robert's table and joined the feast. Soon, they were telling stories about King Richard and the war. They were all false, but Earl Robert and his foresters believed them and loved them. After each story, they laughed and drank 'To the King's safe return' and 'To the end of evil Prince John'. The two knights drank too, but they did not say the words, and they did not laugh.

Then another forester, taller than all the others, entered the hall with a boy. 'That boy is the miller's son,' the thin knight whispered to his older friend. The forester sat the boy down at a table with some other young people. Then he came to Earl Robert's table and whispered something. Earl Robert first looked shocked, then sad, then angry, and then he tried to smile again. 'I'm sorry,' he said to the two knights. 'I'm forgetting my guests. This is William Scathlope, my friend and the leader of my bodyguards.'

Later, Worman led the two knights away to a dark corner and said quietly, 'I hear that it was Robin Hood's right-hand man, Will Scarlet, who took the miller's son away to join Robin Hood yesterday. And now, look, it's Earl Robert's right-hand man, William Scathlope, who has brought the boy to Locksley House. That's strange, isn't it?'

'So,' said Prince John, 'if Will Scarlet and William Scathlope are the same person, then Earl Robert and Robin Hood are also the same person.'

'And he's your enemy and mine,' added the Sheriff. 'He's a traitor and must die!'

***

Next day, the two knights left early and rode like the wind to Nottingham.

'You're right,' shouted Prince John, 'the traitor must die, and then I'll take his name, his land and Locksley House.'

'What will you do with them?' the Sheriff shouted back. 'Sell them?'

'Yes, and then at last I'll have lots of Nottingham gold! But who might pay me well to be the next Earl of Huntingdon?'

'That's easy! Sir Guy has money, but no land. He'll certainly pay.'

'Then Sir Guy will be the new Earl of Huntingdon! But what about the beautiful Lady Marian? Does Sir Guy also want a wife?'

'He does, and he wants Lady Marian! But she's said no four times!'

'No problem,' said Prince John with a horrible smile. 'Lady Marian will marry the Earl of Huntingdon after all – the new Earl of Huntingdon!'

'But first we must stop the marriage of Lady Marian to Earl Robert.'

'I'm sure Sir Guy of Gisborne will happily help do that,' Prince John said. For the first time, the Sheriff saw the Prince laugh.

6 Escape to the forest

While Prince John and the Sheriff were riding back to Nottingham, a happy crowd of people was on its way to Fountains Abbey for the marriage of Earl Robert and Lady Marian.

Old Sir Patrick had no son and was happy with this marriage. He could not imagine a better son-in-law.

Because there were dangers, Earl Robert and the Fitzwalters needed bodyguards – William Scathlope and the foresters. They rode on each side and watched carefully. Farther back, Worman also watched. 'Something is going to happen,' he thought. 'But what, when and where?'

Robert and Marian were not thinking about land or danger. They were looking at each other and thinking about their new life together.

***

The Abbot himself led the wedding service. Soon, Sir Patrick was bringing his daughter forward, and then she and Earl Robert stood together.

The Abbot began to speak. Everybody listened silently. All eyes were on Earl Robert and Lady Marian. Soon the Abbot came to the wonderful words, 'Do you, Robert, take this woman to be your ...?'

And then it happened. The door of the abbey swung open and hit the stone wall with a crash. Everybody in the abbey turned. There at the door was a knight on a tall horse. The foresters reached for their weapons, and the knight shouted, 'In the King's name, put down your weapons!' It was Sir Guy of Gisborne!

He held up a scroll, opened it and started to speak. 'Robert Locksley, also called Robin Hood, I have here the words of Prince John, ruler of all England for his brother King Richard.' He started to read. 'Robert Locksley and Robin Hood are the same man, and so Locksley has broken the King's laws and is a traitor to the King. The name of Earl of Huntingdon is no longer his, and his land and Locksley House are now the King's. He is an outlaw, and he will go with Sir Guy of Gisborne to Nottingham Castle. There he will die as an outlaw.' The harsh words sounded around the abbey. Then there was silence for a moment.

There was very little time. Robin turned to Marian. 'Will you still love me as Robin Hood, and not the Earl of Huntingdon?'

'I will always love you … Robin.'

'Then, please, Sir Patrick, look after my wife for me until we can safely marry.'

Sir Patrick's face was completely white. He realized now that Robert Locksley really was Robin Hood. 'What?' he thought, horrified. 'My daughter almost married the outlaw Robin Hood? This must stop now! If it doesn't, the Fitzwalter family will lose everything, too.' To Robin he said, 'The outlaw Robin Hood can never marry my daughter!'

'When King Richard returns, I will be the Earl of Huntingdon again. You'll see. I promise you.'

In his heart, Sir Patrick hoped that Robin was right. But for

now, Prince John was the ruler, and he had to save his family and land. 'Go! Go while you still can,' he said quickly.
At the door, Sir Guy was looking back and calling his men, 'Quickly! Get the outlaw now – in the abbey!'

***

Robin ran from one end of the abbey to the other in seconds, grabbed a sword from one of his men, leapt up and swung it at Sir Guy. He hit Sir Guy across the head, and only the knight's heavy helmet saved his life. He fell to the floor of the abbey, unconscious.

Robin's men moved fast, too. Close behind Robin, they got to the door at the same time at Sir Guy's men.

Worman went, too. 'If I don't, they'll know I've helped Prince John and the Sheriff,' he thought. At the door, there was a short, fierce fight before the men in green broke through the group of soldiers. Three of the soldiers lay hurt on the ground.

At the abbey gate, Robin turned to his men. 'To those who want to stay with the outlaw Robin Hood, I say welcome to a dangerous life in the forest. But there we'll live like kings, not slaves, and we'll fight evil Prince John, Sir Guy and the Sheriff until King Richard comes home. But, for those who must look after their families, I understand. Go back quickly now, hide in the crowd and stay alive.

While he was speaking, the crowd was coming out of the abbey, jumping over Sir Guy, still unconscious on the abbey floor, and jumping over the soldiers on the ground outside. Everybody was talking, and laughing and shouting at the soldiers. And the soldiers who were still standing shouted back angrily. They wanted revenge.

One of them pointed past the crowd to a man in green who was running back from the abbey gate. 'He's going to try and hide in the crowd!' the soldier shouted. They raised their bows.

The man in green saw this and panicked. 'No! Please! My name is Wor…' It was too late. He fell to the ground with ten arrows in his chest.

Close to the forest, Robin and the others stopped again. Will turned to young Much and said, 'I'm sure Worman was the one who killed your father. He was a traitor!'

'Then it was my job to kill Worman,' Much answered.

'It's better this way. Your hands are clean,' said Will.

'He's paid heavily, too,' Robin said. 'Ten arrows for one.' And he added, 'That's a lesson for Prince John and the Sheriff and Sir Guy to learn.'

They turned and disappeared into the shadows of Sherwood Forest. The last that they heard was when Sir Guy shouted from the abbey door, 'You idiots! You've killed our spy!'

PART 2

HOW THE OUTLAW BAND GREW

1 The first summer

Robin and Will Scarlet led the little group of fifteen men deep, deep into the centre of the forest. They travelled until at last they reached a beautiful place that very few people knew about. The warm evening sun was bright on the grass and flowers along the stream. And at the centre of the little valley grew a wonderful old tree. Robin stood under it and held out his hands. 'Here we'll stay,' he said. 'Here we'll be safe.'

***

Spring changed to summer, and all this time Robin and his band were very busy. They had to build a new life for themselves, and new homes, too, ready for the winter.

And that was not all. The outlaws were also busy on the Great North Road. This, the main route from London to the north, went through the forest for thirty kilometres. Every day, Robin or Will and a few other men watched from the trees as people travelled north or south. But they were interested only in some – the richest and the poorest.

When they saw poor people – perhaps a family on foot with no shoes – they often came down from the trees and did something which soon made them famous. They invited these people to be Robin Hood's guests. They covered their eyes, took them to the camp, and there, they gave them a good meal. They also asked about the cause of their problems. Often, it was the evil masters of Nottingham, and the outlaws became angrier and angrier. At the end, Robin always helped his guests before they continued their journey – a present of money, perhaps, or food or shoes and clothes.

Of course, these things had to come from somewhere, and the outlaws themselves needed things, too. This was where the richest travellers helped a lot. Sometimes the outlaws just stopped them and politely took what they needed. Sometimes there was a fight – and then they took what they needed. Sometimes Robin invited rich travellers to dinner – just like the poor people. But there was a difference. Afterwards, Robin always smiled and said, 'Now, I'm sorry, but could you please pay for your food?' And then again ... his men took what they needed. When Robin said goodbye, he always said, politely, 'Thank you. You're helping us to help people who are really poor.'

This was another thing that made the outlaws famous. But in Nottingham, it made the Sheriff and Sir Guy very angry! Prince John, too, far away in London. And there seemed to be a new story every week!

***

The little band of outlaws was growing. Other outlaws came. People who were suffering under cruel lords like the Sheriff of Nottingham came. And often they brought their families. By September, sixty people were living in the secret forest valley.

This was a good thing, Robin felt. Soon, perhaps, with two or three hundred men who all hated Prince John and the greedy lords, they could really attack the Sheriff. But there were also problems. First, these people – women and children, too, and not just men – all needed food. And they needed more huts before winter. And many of the new people needed to learn how to live in the forest. And before they could attack the Sheriff, most of the new people needed to learn to fight. They needed to train with swords and bows and arrows. Robin needed more people who could help.

2 How Little John joined the band

When Robin wanted to think about these problems, he liked walking alone by the river. He always gave these instructions. 'If you need me, blow your horn. And if I need you, I'll blow mine.'

One day, Robin was walking there when he found a fallen tree across the water. He decided to cross and walk on the other side, but as he started, a huge man with a big beard appeared at the other end.

'Hello, stranger,' Robin called. 'We can't both go at the same time, so I'll go first. I'll be quick.'

'Not quick enough for me,' the stranger called back. 'So I'll go first.'

Both men started to cross the bridge at the same time. 'Go back, little man,' shouted the big stranger. 'Or do you want to have a cold bath?' And he added, 'After a good bang on the head with this!' He waved a thick, two-metre staff at Robin and laughed.

Robin could not say no to something like that. 'Maybe *you're* going to have a cold bath!' he shouted back. He went back, put down his horn and weapons, went to a tree by the river and cut a strong staff for himself.

The two men moved towards each other. Robin was not a small man, but the stranger was amazing. He was a giant, and he looked very strong. 'I just hope I'm better with a staff than him,' Robin thought.

'Well, little man, can you swim well?' the stranger laughed.

Robin said nothing. He was really angry now!

The giant swung his staff at Robin's head, but Robin hit back and nearly sent the stranger straight into the water. 'Not bad,' the giant said, 'but not good enough!' He took a step forward and swung again.

The fight went on and on, and after ten minutes, both men were tired. Then Robin attacked again. But his foot slipped, and the stranger's staff quickly pushed him into the river below.

The fast water quickly carried him away, his head crashed into a rock, and everything went black. His unconscious body slowly sank.

***

Robin felt a hand around his arm. Somebody was pulling him out of the water. His head hurt and he was coughing water. 'Good, you'll be all right now,' he heard.

Robin opened his eyes and looked up. The stranger was looking back at him. He grinned and said, 'You're better at fighting than swimming.'

Robin finally stopped coughing and said, 'Thanks for saving my life.'

'Well, I couldn't let a good fighter like you just die in the water. Nobody has ever been able to fight me for so long before.'

'Well, you won, so now you can cross the river and go on your way.' Robin slowly stood up. 'But first, please be my guest and eat with me.'

'Thank you, but I must tell you that I eat a lot!'

'No problem.' Friends now, they went back across the tree to Robin's side. There, Robin picked up his horn and other things. Then he asked, 'Why are you travelling so far from the road and so deep in the forest?'

'I'm looking for Robin Hood. I want to join him and help him fight the Sheriff of Nottingham.'

Robin was very pleased. Here was another real fighter. He could help train the new people back at the camp. Wonderful!

He said, 'It's a lucky day for both of us. You've found Robin Hood!'

'You? Robin Hood?' The stranger grinned. 'You're a good fighter, but you're not big enough to be Robin Hood. People say that Robin Hood is a giant, so I'm looking for a man who's as big as me – a man who can even frighten the Sheriff of Nottingham and evil Prince John!'

'I tell you, you're talking to Robin Hood,' Robin said. But the stranger laughed, and Robin started to get angry again.

'Give me some proof,' the stranger said.

'All right.' Robin took his horn and blew hard. 'Your proof will be here very soon,' he said. 'And now, let's go to the camp. I'm hungry.'

A little later, they heard a small sound from bushes near the path. 'An animal for lunch,' said the stranger, and he raised his staff, ready to attack.

But no. He was suddenly looking into the eyes of a line of men, all in green, and all with bows and arrows that were pointing at his heart.

Robin held up his hand. 'It's all right,' he said. 'He's a friend, and he's coming to eat with us. I hope he's going to stay, too.'

His men relaxed. 'Thank God you're all right, Robin,' said one of them – Will Scarlet. He smiled.

'So ...' the stranger turned to Robin. 'It seems you really are Robin Hood. I can only say that your name and fame are a lot bigger than you are!'

Robin smiled. 'Now you know my name, so tell us yours.'

'They call me John Little.'

'Well, since you worry so much about people's size, I'm going to give you a new name: Little John.' The others laughed.

The big man first seemed annoyed, but then he grinned and started to enjoy the joke. 'All right, Little John it is,' he agreed.

That was how Little John joined the outlaws and got his name. And Robin was right. Little John was a great help with the new people. He also became as close a friend to Robin as Will Scarlet was.

3 How Robin helped Sir Richard of Lee

Barnsdale Forest in Yorkshire was another of England's forests, and Robin travelled there with a small group just before Midsummer's Day. They went for a good reason. Sherwood might not always be safe, and they needed to find other safe places – like Barnsdale.

They found a good place for a secret camp and then thought about dinner. 'Let's go and find a deer,' said Will Scarlet.

'Yes, but let's also find a dinner guest or two,' said Robin. 'Little John, find us a fat abbot, or a rich lord, or a proud knight in expensive armour. Somebody who can pay us well for dinner.'

So Little John, Much and another man went west towards the road. Meanwhile, Robin and the others started looking for their dinner.

***

The three men waited behind bushes by the road. Minutes and then hours passed, and Little John got worried. 'If we don't find somebody soon,' he thought, 'it'll be night, and there won't be anybody on the road.'

But finally they saw a tall, thin man in armour on a horse. 'At last! A knight!' whispered Little John. 'He'll be our guest.' But when they looked more closely, something seemed wrong. The man's head was down, and he seemed sad, or worried.

There was another thing. The coat over his armour was old and thin, and the armour itself was old and rusty. 'Well,' whispered Little John, 'he doesn't look very rich, but he's the richest we'll find today, so it has to be him.'

They moved out into the road. 'Good evening, sir. We have an invitation for you to eat with our master this evening.'

The knight stopped and looked at the three men in green. 'Who are you and who's your master?'

'He's Robin Hood, and we're his men,' Little John replied.

'That's a famous name, and people say he's a good man because he helps the poor. I'll happily eat with Robin Hood.'

The foresters looked at each other. This was not the answer of a knight like Sir Guy of Gisborne! Finally, Little John said, 'Come, sir. Robin is waiting.'

***

'Welcome,' said Robin. 'Please, tell us your name.'

'I'm Sir Richard of Lee,' said the knight.

'Well, Sir Richard, dinner's ready, so come and eat.'

As they ate, the stranger asked a lot about life in the forest, but he did not talk about himself.

At the end, he said, 'Thank you, Robin. I haven't eaten as well as this for many months. I'd like to invite you to Lee Castle and do the same for you. But ...,' and now Sir Richard just whispered quietly to himself, 'that'll never again be possible.'

'Well, thank you, Sir Richard, but with people like yourself, we just ask for money. We need money from the rich so that we can help the poor.'

'I'm sorry, Robin, but I'm not rich. I have almost nothing.'

'How can that be true? Tell me: exactly how much have you got?'

'Just two shillings.'

'If you really have so little, I won't take it. But first, I'm sorry, we must look in your bags. We must be sure you're as poor as you say. Much, could you do that, please?'

Much looked carefully but found only two shillings – exactly two. Robin turned to his guest. 'It's clear you're an honest man, and it's also clear you have problems. Let's have another drink and talk. Maybe I can help.'

***

Sir Richard began. 'I have lands that bring me 500 pounds a year. But my family and I are going to lose everything tomorrow, at midday on Midsummer's Day.'

'But how have you lost so much? Why?'

'Because of the cruel Abbot of St Mary's Abbey. Three years ago my son Edward went to the war with King Richard. He fought well, but he was caught, and six months ago I was forced to pay a ransom of 1,000 pounds.'

'That's a lot of money.'

'Yes, and I had only 600. So I went to the Abbot for 400 more. He let me have the money, but I have to give it back by tomorrow.'

'Or the good Abbot will take everything?'

'That's right. I saved hard and I had just enough. Then, three weeks ago, Prince John's soldiers came with a man that they call Sir Guy of Gisborne, and they took everything. Everything. A special tax, they said.'

Robin's eyes burned angrily when he heard that name again.

'Anyway,' Sir Richard went on. 'I was on my way to St

Mary's Abbey today – it's just ten miles from here. I want to ask for more time. The answer will be no, but I have to try.'

Robin said to Much, 'Bring me the bag from my horse, please.' He turned back to Sir Richard. 'It's a lot of money, but I'd like to help. If I let you have the money, will you pay me back a year from now?'

'Robin, are you mad? You can't really mean that!'

'I can and I do.' Much came back with the bag, and Robin gave Sir Richard the money that he needed – almost everything in the bag. 'And now, Sir Richard, stay with us tonight. Leave early tomorrow and you'll reach St Mary's Abbey before midday.'

Sir Richard was very, very grateful. When he said goodbye next day, he said, 'Robin, you're the best man in the world. And I promise I'll be here with your money at midday on Midsummer's Day a year from today.'

***

At St Mary's Abbey, the people who lived on the abbey's lands and worked on the abbey's many farms were coming and paying their rents. The Abbot sat high on a golden throne in the great hall of the abbey, and his assistant, the Prior of the abbey, sat at a table below him. The Prior waited there, a pen in his hand, and the abbey's huge book of accounts open in front of him. One by one, the people came, bowed to the Abbot and then moved on to the Prior and the giant book. Some paid money, and others paid with animals.

A few could not pay – sometimes because of illness, for example. This was when the Abbot really enjoyed himself. 'You must give the abbey everything that you have,' he always shouted at these poor, frightened people, 'and then leave the abbey's lands – by tomorrow!'

Sometimes, people knelt and begged for kindness: 'Please! How will my family live? Please, give me some time, my Lord!'

But the answer was always the same. 'It's too late for that now. Why didn't you think about it before? Now get out!'

It was almost midday. The Prior looked at his book and pointed at a name. 'There's one more very important man who must come today, by midday.'

'You mean Sir Richard of Lee, of course.'

'I do, my Lord.'

'And it'll soon be midday. Then his castle and his lands will be mine ... the abbey's, I mean.' The Abbot laughed.

'But he may still come with the money,' the Prior said.

'No, I don't think so. My friend Sir Guy of Gisborne took everything that Sir Richard had three weeks ago. No, Sir Richard won't appear today. Ha-ha-ha!'

***

The Abbot suddenly stopped laughing. A tall, thin man was standing at the door to the hall. It was Sir Richard.

The knight came forward and knelt. 'Well?' said the Abbot. 'Have you brought the money?'

'As you can see, I'm a poor man. Prince John's men took everything that I had three weeks ago.'

'Lee Castle really is mine!' the Abbot thought. He wanted to laugh but instead shouted, 'So why are you here if you've brought no money?'

'I've come to beg for time. If you give me six months, I'll pay.'

'This is rubbish,' the Abbot shouted back.

'But listen, my Lord Abbot, please. Just think. My son was caught while he was fighting for the Christian Church in the Holy Land. So isn't it right and Christian for the Church to help a little and give me time?'

Around the hall people whispered, 'Sir Richard is right.'

But the Abbot shook his head and answered, 'No, no, no. We agreed a date, and a knight must always keep his promise.'

'How can a lord of the Christian Church be so cruel to a Christian knight? This is very wrong, very wrong.'

'Oh, stop it, stop it!' the Abbot said. He looked up at the sky through the hall's south window. 'The sun is reaching its highest point, Sir Richard. So, since you have no money, please just give me the castle keys.'

'Ah, but you're wrong, cruel Abbot. I didn't say I have no money. And here it is.' Sir Richard stood up and slowly took four bags from under his coat and put them on the Prior's table, one by one.

The Abbot's mouth fell open. His eyes were like dinner plates.

'Go on,' Sir Richard said to the Prior. 'Open them and count the money.' He looked at the Abbot. 'Now the world will know you're a cruel man and not a true Christian. This story will be famous all over England.'

Around the hall, the people whispered quietly, 'Yes!'

The Abbot's face was bright red: 'Bu ... Bu ... But ...' Then at last, he found a few words: 'Get out of here! Get out! Get out!' he screamed.

But Sir Richard was already going.

PART 3

THE GREAT FIGHT

1 The rescue

It was a cold March, but Robin Hood's band were alive and well and looking forward to spring.

One morning, when there was still a little snow on the ground, Robin stood and looked across the busy camp. There were now nearly 200 people there – men, women and children – and every day a few more came.

All of them had their own stories about the cruel Sheriff and even crueller Sir Guy. The Sheriff was taking everything now, and the people had no money, no food, nothing. Anybody who killed a deer for food – or even a rabbit – was hanged. Nobody was safe.

It was time for the morning practice – practice with swords, staffs and bows and arrows – because now these people in the forest wanted to fight and get back their homes and lives. Robin looked around. Nearest him was Little John's group. Robin smiled as the huge man shouted, grinned, laughed and helped his pupils. Robin quietly thought, 'When these people came, most were weak and ill and without hope. But now look at them! This year, we're really going to surprise the Sheriff and Sir Guy.'

***

That night, fires were burning brightly across the valley. Around one of them, the fire lit the faces of Robin and his closest friends as they discussed plans for the new year. 'This year,' Robin said, 'we must stop hiding and start attacking.'

'That's right,' Little John said. 'But how? And when?'

Just then, an old woman was brought to the fire. She fell at Robin's feet. 'Please save my little grandsons,' she cried. 'The Sheriff is going to hang them tomorrow.'

'Why? What have they done?'

'They took an egg – just one – from the castle hen house.'

Robin looked around, and everybody nodded grimly. To the old woman he said, 'Something will be done.'

***

A drum sounded as three boys were led to the platform in the town square. A large crowd watched angrily, as ropes were put around the boys' necks. Their grandmother was frantic. Where was Robin?

The Sheriff went up the steps. With him was Sir Guy, and he was pulling a beautiful woman by the arm. She tried to pull away but could not. It was Lady Marian, now the fiancée of the new Earl of Huntingdon, and she hated him.

The Sheriff shouted, 'You people, remember. Nobody steals from me, and that includes children!'

He nodded to the hangman.

The grandmother screamed, 'No!'

Near the platform, someone in a cloak shouted. The air was suddenly full of arrows from every side. Soldiers fell, and the fat Sheriff half-ran, half-fell down the steps to hide. Guy let go of Marian and grabbed his sword.

Robin and his men quickly took off their cloaks and ran up the stairs onto the platform. And people below jumped up, grabbed Guy's legs and pulled him down.

Marian took out a knife and cut the boys' ropes. But Guy saw this and shouted, 'You'll be sorry for that when you're mine, Marian!'

2 How Marian escaped to Robin

'Father, I won't marry Guy of Gisborne,' Marian said angrily.

'We can't stop the marriage now,' old Lord Fitzwalter said. 'He's furious because you helped those boys. He's so angry that he wants you under his control right now.'

'He wants a prisoner, not a wife! He's horrible!'

'He's riding here from Nottingham right now. He wants to plan everything today and marry you on Saturday.'

'I won't see him!' She ran out of the great hall and up the stone stairs to her room. 'I must escape to Robin in the forest,' she thought. 'But how? And there's so little time!'

Then she had an idea.

Sir Guy arrived. 'I must see my bride,' he said.

Fitzwalter looked grim. 'Call Lady Marian,' he told a servant.

The servant returned after ten minutes. 'I can't find her anywhere.'

Meanwhile, a person in boy's clothes was walking towards Sherwood Forest. 'Will I find Robin Hood?' Marian wondered, 'And will he welcome me?'

***

Robin was standing at the edge of the forest. The Sheriff's spies were everywhere, so he was wearing a heavy cloak with a large hood. He saw the boy on his way towards him, and he pulled the hood lower. 'I'm looking for Robin Hood,' the boy said.

'Many people are looking for that criminal,' Robin replied cautiously.

'Don't call him that!' Marian said angrily, her hand on her sword.

'A child shouldn't be here near criminals like Robin Hood.'

'I'm not a child, and he's not a criminal!' Marian attacked suddenly and cut Robin's left hand.

Robin had to fight back – or die. They fought hard, but Robin was stronger, and the stranger's sword finally fell. 'Not bad for a boy,' Robin said.

'A woman, you mean!' Marian said, and she shook her long hair loose.

'Marian?' Robin stared as he slowly pulled back his hood.

Marian gasped. 'Robin! My Robin!'

They held each other for a long time. It was almost two years since that terrible day at Fountains Abbey when Robin escaped to the forest. Two years! There was a lot to talk about as they walked slowly into the forest together, hand in hand.

'Now,' Robin thought, 'my band is complete. Together, we can do anything. We can beat the Sheriff, Sir Guy, Prince John – anybody!'

3 When Sir Richard of Lee met Robin again

It was the day before Midsummer, a year since Sir Richard first met Robin. Very early, he left Lee Castle with ten men, the money and lots of large bundles – a very special present for Robin and his band.

'We must be there at midday tomorrow,' Sir Richard thought. They travelled fast, stopped by the road that night, and left early again next day. By 11.00, they were in Barnsdale town, only a mile from the forest. But there something forced Sir Richard to stop.

There was a festival in the town that day and the big event was a wrestling competition. For the winner, there were two wonderful prizes – a beautiful white horse and a large barrel of wine. A lot of men wanted the prizes, but one man was winning every fight.

People were shouting at him angrily, and Sir Richard asked an old man why. 'He's a stranger, and people want a Barnsdale man to win our expensive prizes. People want the winner to be a local man.'

'But isn't the competition open to everybody, local or not?'

'True, but if the stranger wins, I'm afraid our young men will kill him. They'll never let him have the prizes.'

The stranger won his last fight. The crowd roared angrily and people started attacking him with sticks and stones.

Sir Richard and his men pushed through the crowd on their horses. He shouted, 'This man is a stranger, but he's won fairly, so you must be fair, too. Now listen, here's an idea. I'll buy the winner's wine, and we'll all drink together. All right? Stranger, is five shillings for your wine a fair price?'

'Very fair, sir.' The young man was pleased to have a friend.

Soon, the whole town was happily drinking. Everybody was becoming the stranger's friend!

Sir Richard suddenly looked up at the sun: it was already after midday, and the meeting place was still miles away in the forest! 'I've broken the most important promise of my life!' he thought. 'Quickly!' he shouted. 'We must ride like the wind!' In a minute, they were gone.

***

Robin and Will looked up at the sun. It was after midday, and Sir Richard was still not there. 'I'm surprised,' said Robin. 'Maybe he's ill.'

Will said, 'Maybe he isn't planning to give back the money.'

Most of the others thought that Will was right, but Little John disagreed. 'No!' he said. 'Sir Richard is honest. He'll be here soon.'

'Well,' said Robin. 'Let's break into two groups. Little John, Will and Much, please stay here and watch the road. When Sir Richard comes, bring him to our camp. And,' he added, 'if you see one or two rich travellers, bring them for dinner, too.' He turned to the others in the group. 'Everybody else, let's find a deer, ready for our feast tonight with Sir Richard.'

***

After half an hour, there was still no Sir Richard. Then Little John heard horses and voices. Was this Sir Richard and his men? No. These people were coming from the direction of St Mary's Abbey. Little John looked. There were two monks on horses and about twenty guards on foot, all with swords and bows. 'There are our rich guests,' he whispered.

'And with all those guards, perhaps they really are carrying a lot of money,' Will whispered back.

'But what are we going to do about the guards?' Much asked.

'Follow me. Do what I do,' Little John said. Then, when the travellers were twenty metres away, he walked quickly to the middle of the road with his bow and arrow ready to shoot. The others did the same. 'Stop!' he said. 'Our arrows are pointing straight between your eyes, and we never miss.'

'Who are you?' asked the older monk. (He was the Prior of St Mary's Abbey, the man who wrote the rents in the great book of accounts.)

'We're Robin Hood's men and he's invited you to dinner.'

The travellers and their guards went white. The guards started to look at the bushes along the road. There must be more than just these three men, they thought. The Prior tried to look brave and said, 'You can't stop us. There are just three of you and we have twenty guards.'

Little John laughed. 'Your guards don't agree. They're looking for more of us in the bushes, and they're right. There are fifty men no more than ten metres from you. If I tell them, they'll shoot, and your guards will die. So please come quietly and enjoy your dinner.'

Nobody moved. Then Little John took his hand from his bow and slowly raised it. 'When my hand falls, they'll shoot,' he said. That was enough for the guards. They all turned and ran away.

Much led the Prior and his assistant away on their horses. Will followed with an arrow that was pointing at the monks' backs. Little John stayed near the road. 'I know Sir Richard

will be here soon,' he said. 'He's an honest man. I'm sure.' But even he was starting to wonder.

***

'I'm very pleased to see you,' Robin said politely to his new guests. 'Am I right that you're from St Mary's Abbey?'

The Prior nodded miserably. 'Well, you're very welcome. You're a bit early for dinner, so come and have a drink first.'

The monks grimly got off their horses and Much took these away. He felt the bags on the backs of the horses, and they were heavy. He went to Robin and whispered to him.

Robin's men brought wine. 'Drink,' he said, and the monks drank, unhappily. 'Oh, and could you pay for dinner now? It'll save time later.'

'We have almost nothing with us – just a few shillings,' said the Prior.

'Well, if that's true, I won't take it. You can't travel without money. And you're men of the Church, so I'm sure you're being honest.'

The Prior went red. 'But,' Robin went on, 'you don't mind if we quickly check your bags, do you?'

'No! You can't! You mustn't.'

'Oh, but we can and we must. Much! Please do it.'

Five minutes later, 800 pounds in gold and silver lay in front of Robin. 'Well,' said Robin. 'St Mary's Abbey is kind. Here's the 400 pounds that I gave a year ago and 400 more in interest. Very kind!'

'That's money for Prince John. If you take it, he'll kill you!'

Robin grinned. 'Maybe, maybe not.' he said. 'Meanwhile, your dinner will be the best that we can make here in the forest.'

'We can't fight you,' the Prior said. 'But we certainly won't eat with you. You're the world's most horrible thieves. Give us our horses and we'll go!'

Robin said, 'Well, if you're sure you must go, then you must.' He turned to Much and Will. 'Please take these good men back to the road.'

***

Little John heard more horses. And yes, it was Sir Richard! He was very pleased. He noticed that Sir Richard was still in that old suit of armour. 'He's clearly saved every penny that he could,' he thought.

'Little John! It's wonderful to see you again!' Sir Richard said. 'I'm very sorry I'm late,' he went on, 'but there was a good reason.'

'No problem. Robin will be very pleased to see you.'

And he was. Most of all, he was pleased that Sir Richard was honest and kept his promises. Then Sir Richard explained the reason for the delay, and Robin was even more pleased. 'You helped somebody who badly needed help. You did the right thing.'

'Next,' Sir Richard said, 'here's a present for all of you. He called his own men over, and each brought a long bundle, and put it down in front of Robin. 'Open them,' he said to Robin.

Robin opened the first one. Inside were ten beautiful bows. 'I believe they're the best in England,' Sir Richard said. 'A hundred of them.' He called to his men again, and they brought more bundles. Robin opened one. Inside were arrows. 'Twenty for each bow, Robin,' Sir Richard said.

Robin and his men gasped. 'This is a wonderful present – and very expensive,' Robin said at last. He picked up a bow and an arrow and pointed at a tree 100 metres away. 'The lowest leaf,' he said. The arrow flew through the air and cut the leaf from the tree. The leaf fell slowly to the ground. 'Wonderful! These weapons will be a great help.'

'Good, and now we come to the main thing. The money.' Sir Richard opened the large bags on the back of his horse. 'Here you are.'

'Stop, Sir Richard,' Robin said. 'Two monks have just visited us, and they've given back the 400 pounds – and a lot more, too! Anyway, you've already given us all these weapons. So no, keep the money.'

'I can't. I must keep my promise.'

'You have kept your promise – and more ... Keep the money for your family and your men. But please, please, do one thing.'

'What's that, Robin?'

'Buy yourself a new suit of armour!' Everybody laughed.

4 The silver arrow

In London, Prince John was furious. Every day, there was a new story or song about Robin Hood! He wanted to take his whole army north and finally kill Robin and all his men.

But that idea was too expensive. And anyway, he mustn't make Robin Hood an even bigger hero. Think! Robin Hood and a few men against an army! Imagine all the songs about that! No, there must be another way.

Then he had the perfect idea. He called monks from Westminster Abbey, and they wrote copies of this letter to all the lords in the north.

My Lord of ...

I plan to visit Nottingham in August and I want to invite you to a great festival there for the people of the north. The main event will be an archery competition to find the best archer in the north. The prize will be a silver arrow a metre long, and a hundred pounds in gold. Please send out this message to all your towns and villages and invite the best archers to Nottingham on the last Saturday in August.

***

Robin and the others soon heard about the great competition. 'It's a trap, Robin,' said Marian. 'You mustn't go.'

'Marian is right,' said Will Scarlet. 'Don't go.'

'Ah, but I can't say no to a challenge like this!' said Robin. 'I'll go in disguise as a forester from Barnsdale Forest.'

'Well,' said Will, 'if you go, I'll go too and guard you.' Little John said the same thing. Robin tried to say no, but everybody wanted to go with him. So then he decided he could not go: 'It's too dangerous for my men,' he thought. 'All right,' he said to Marian and the others, 'I won't go.'

But later he had another idea when everybody was practising their fighting skills. 'We're good now,' he thought. 'Good enough to fight a battle. And perhaps this competition is the perfect chance to beat the Sheriff and Prince John, both at the same time.'

***

The great day came. Prince John was paying for all the food and drink, and thousands were there. He thought, 'It seems I'm paying for a whole army anyway! I only hope it'll buy me Robin Hood.'

At the end of the afternoon, there were just three men still in the competition. Prince John, with the Sheriff and Sir Guy, looked from one to another of the archers. There was a giant who said he was from the Wirral, a forest in the west. Then there was a smaller, younger man from Barnsdale Forest. Finally, there was a quiet, older man from Sherwood.

'The Sherwood man isn't Robin Hood, I'm sure,' said Sir Guy.

'But I know who he is,' answered Prince John, and he turned to the Sheriff. 'Do you remember Locksley House? And the man who arrived with the miller's son?'

'You mean ... William Scathlope? Will Scarlet?'

'Yes, and if that's Will Scarlet, his master isn't far away.' Their eyes turned to the man from Barnsdale. 'And,' said Sir Guy quietly, 'they say that his other closest friend is a giant.' They looked at the third man.

Another man was looking carefully at each archer. He was also hearing names that were whispered under the shouts and cheers – 'Will Scarlet' ... 'Little John' ... 'Robin Hood'. 'So there are real people behind all the stories,' he thought. 'And wonderful archers they are, too!'

This man was in a knight's armour, but he wore no crest and just stood with the ordinary people, away from Prince John and the other lords and ladies. He had a red-gold beard and blue eyes that laughed and at the same time saw deep into people. 'But,' he thought, 'are they also the wonderful heroes that the stories say they are – or just ordinary thieves?'

The older man shot from 230 metres. He hit the white outside circle but missed the small, red centre. Then it was the giant's turn, and he hit the line between the white and the red. Finally, the younger man came forward. The crowd watched silently. The arrow flew from the bow, climbed a little, fell a little and ... hit the exact centre. By now, nearly all the crowd knew that this was Robin Hood, and five thousand men, women and children cheered and shouted and ran towards him and the other two.

With the huge crowd around him, Robin came over to Prince John, the Sheriff and Sir Guy. The knight with no crest turned, and his eyes caught the eyes of another knight, a younger man – his servant perhaps. Both men moved closer to Robin. They wanted to hear him and Prince John.

***

Robin did not kneel in front of Prince John. Instead, he looked straight into the Prince's eyes and said, 'My prizes, please.'

Sir Guy hissed. 'Robin Hood, you're going to die for this!' He raised his arm, ready to call his soldiers.

But Prince John stopped him. 'Don't be an idiot!' Then he whispered, 'You only have fifty men here, and there are thousands of people around Robin Hood. If your men try to take Robin Hood now, we'll all die. Just wait, and we'll catch him later.' He really, really wished he had his army with him!

'My prizes, please,' Robin said again.

'Yes. Enjoy them for the rest of your life,' Prince John said coldly, and he thought, '...your very short life.' He called, and a man came forward with the arrow and the gold. 'Give the prizes to this forest thief,' he said.

Robin spoke. 'Yes, I'm a thief, but I only take from the rich. To the poor, I give. I give back to the poor the things that the rich have stolen.' The crowd roared. 'Things like this gold.' He opened the bag and threw the money to the people. The crowd roared again, louder, and thousands of hands reached for the coins.

The Sheriff gasped. 'You cannot speak to your ruler like this!'

'My ruler is King Richard, and nobody else.' The crowd roared again, loudest of all.

***

'And now it's time to go back to the forest,' Robin said.

'We'll go, too, and guard you,' many people said, and hundreds went with Robin and the others. They pushed past Sir Guy's few soldiers easily.

'Where are the rest of Sir Guy's men?' Robin wondered.

'Where are the rest of Robin Hood's band?' Sir Guy wondered. 'Because today I'm going to find them and kill them. All of them – men, women and children!' He turned towards the Castle, pulled out his sword and waved it. A giant red flag rose above the Castle.

The two strangers in armour went quickly to their horses at the end of the field. 'Let's go quickly,' said the older man. He pointed to the red flag. 'Something's going to happen, and we need to be in the right place at the right time.'

***

Sir Richard of Lee was riding fast from the north through Sherwood Forest. Behind him were 50 men.

They came out of the forest. The road ahead went past fields, woods and a small village, and then to Nottingham two miles away. Between Nottingham and the village, they saw a large crowd of people. Behind the village houses, they also saw the light of the sun on metal – swords and armour. 'Soldiers!' said Sir Richard. 'Let's go!' he shouted.

***

Near the village, Marian was hiding behind a large tree by the road. She was watching the soldiers and also the crowd of people on the road. The soldiers were ready to attack, and the crowd was getting close. She could clearly see Robin, Will and Little John.

Then she heard horses back along the road behind her. She turned. It was Sir Richard. Much, the miller's son was behind the next tree. They looked at each other, Marian with a question in her eyes. Much nodded and whispered, 'Yes!' Marian moved quickly out into the road. She stopped them and put a finger to her mouth. 'Come quietly,' she whispered.

Sir Richard understood. He and his men got off their horses and moved forward quietly on the grass by the road.

***

Robin guessed that the soldiers were hiding in the village. He turned to the crowd. 'Thank you all,' he said. 'You've helped Will, Little John and me leave Nottingham safely, but now we're close to Sherwood, so please go home. If Sir Guy finds you here, he'll know that you were helping us, and that'll be dangerous for you and your families. So go now. Please.'

The people did not want to leave, but finally they turned back.

Robin and the others silently walked the last 200 metres to the village. This was the most dangerous time. Each hoped that the rest of their band were ready. Each watched the little houses and the low walls around them.

In fact, the attack started from behind. The people on their way back to Nottingham had to throw themselves off the road as Sir Guy and his soldiers rode straight through them.

Then came the attack from the soldiers in the village – hundreds of them. The air was suddenly full of arrows. Robin, Little John and Will ran to a small hut. From there, they started to shoot back as fast as they could. For a moment, the Sheriff's men stopped coming forward.

But not for long. Robin and the others needed help soon.

The help came – and much more than Robin was expecting. With Much, Marian and the army of men and women in forest green came Sir Richard and his band. The Sheriff's men turned, shocked. Suddenly, they were facing not just three dangerous enemies, but three hundred!

Then it was the turn of Sir Guy and his band of soldiers. From along the road behind them came a shout: 'For King Richard!' The two strangers in armour came riding with their swords high in the air, and with them was the whole crowd from Nottingham. And as the people came, they took stones from the walls along the road and threw them at the soldiers.

The battle was short but terrible. Soon the road was covered with bodies and red with blood. The soldiers who were still alive started trying to run away, but there was nowhere to go. The attacks came from every side. The last man still on his horse was Sir Guy. He turned and turned and cut down men and women until his sword was red with blood. 'Fight! Fight like men!' he shouted at the few soldiers still around him.

It was at this moment that Much the miller's son took out an arrow that was different from all the others that he had. It was an arrow that was black with soot. It hit Sir Guy in the eye so hard that it went straight through him to the back of his head and threw him from his horse into the air. He was dead before he hit the ground.

Much dropped his bow and he himself fell to the ground. He was shaking all over and could not stop. He covered his face in his hands. 'Now at last,' he cried, 'you've paid for the evil day that you came to my father's mill.'

***

'Father?' It was the younger of the two strangers.

Sir Richard was helping a man who was hurt. When he heard the voice, he thought he was dreaming. He slowly turned. This was not the son that he remembered from three years before – a thin, young boy. This was a man, but ... yes ... the eyes ... the voice ...: 'Edward?' he whispered.

'Yes, Father, it really is me. Thanks to the ransom money that you sent, I've come home.'

Father and son held each other. 'Thank God!' said Sir Richard.

***

Robin turned to the other stranger. 'Thank you for your help. You and your young friend and the crowd arrived at exactly the right moment.'

The stranger laughed. 'Well,' he said, 'I know about that sort of thing from the war in the Holy Land.'

'It's good to meet somebody who has fought with King Richard,' Robin said. 'Tell me, is the King alive? Is he safe? Where is he?'

'I can tell you that he's alive, yes, and he's safe because he's with friends, and he's also now in England.' The stranger's eyes met the eyes of Edward, still with his arm around his father. They smiled.

Edward spoke. 'Don't you know?' he said. 'This is King Richard!'

Robin looked back at the older stranger, and he knew it was true. He knelt, but the King quickly said, 'Get up, Robin Hood. Now that I see what's happened here and what you've done, it's I who should kneel, not you!'

Edward explained. 'King Richard is travelling secretly around England. He wants to find out about people's lives under Prince John.

The King added, 'I heard that life was bad for the ordinary people. But it's much worse than I thought. I now have to take the country back from John and evil lords like the Sheriff of Nottingham.'

'What will you do with them, my Lord?' asked Robin.

The King looked away, and his eyes were not laughing now. 'I'm not sure,' he said heavily. 'For now,' he went on, 'we'll send these men back to Nottingham with a message for my brother.' He pointed at the five frightened soldiers who were still alive. 'I'll meet him in the archery fields tomorrow. And first, we'll talk, brother to brother.'

Then he smiled. 'But that's tomorrow's problem. Today, I want you to take me to your camp in the forest, and I want to meet all the people that I've heard about. The stories also say that you're eating a lot of the King's deer – my deer! – so I'd like to taste one, too, please.'

'Of course, my Lord. Whatever we have is yours.'

'In Sherwood, it seems that whatever I have is yours!' Everybody laughed with the King.

***

The rest of that day was both happy and terribly sad. Nearly all the Sheriff's soldiers were dead, but some of Robin's and Sir Robert's people and the Nottingham crowd were dead too, and many more were badly hurt.

And King Richard was shocked by the stories that he later heard about the evil of the Sheriff, Sir Guy and his brother. 'My poor, poor country,' he thought again and again.

One of the stories was about the marriage of Robin and Marian. 'But do you still want to marry this terrible outlaw?' the King asked Marian.

'More and more,' she answered. 'But my father says that I can never marry the outlaw Robin Hood.'

'But Robin Hood is in fact Robert Locksley, and of course Robert Locksley is and always was the real Earl of Huntingdon.'

'Thank you, my Lord,' Robin and Marian said together.

'This is one story that will have a clear and happy end,' the King went on. 'Tomorrow, the two of you must go to Lord Fitzwalter and tell him this news. Then, a week from today, we will all go to Fountains Abbey and finish the wedding that began so long ago!'

VOCABULARY

A

a: 500 pounds a year 500 Pfund im Jahr
abbot ['æbət] Abt
account [ə'kaʊnt]: **book of accounts** Rechnungsbuch
ahead [ə'hed]: **the way ahead** den Weg voraus **the road ahead** die Straße vor ihnen
all over: all over England überall in England; **all over his body** am ganzen Körper
amazing [ə'meɪzɪŋ] verblüffend
anger ['æŋgə] Wut
annoyed [ə'nɔɪd] ärgerlich
archer ['ɑːtʃə] (Bogen-)Schütze
archery ['ɑːtʃəri] Bogenschießen
armour ['ɑːmə] Rüstung
army ['ɑːmi] Armee
around [ə'raʊnd] überall
arrow ['ærəʊ] Pfeil
(to) **attack** [ə'tæk] angreifen

B

badly dringend; schwer
barrel of wine [ˌbærəl əv 'waɪn] Weinfass
battle ['bætl] Schlacht, Kampf
beard [bɪəd] Bart
(to) **beg (for kindness)** [beg] (um Gnade) bitten
better at: You're better at fighting du kannst besser kämpfen
bow [bəʊ] Bogen
(to) **bow** [baʊ] sich verbeugen
bundle ['bʌndl] Bündel
(to) **bury** ['beri] begraben
bush ['bʊʃ] Busch, Strauch
by bis

C

camp [kæmp] Lager
cart [kɑːt] Karren
cattle ['kætl] Vieh, Rinder
cautious ['kɔːʃəs] vorsichtig
certainly ['sɜːtnli] sicherlich
challenge ['tʃælɪndʒ] Herausforderung
cheer [tʃɪə] Jubel
chest [tʃest] Brust
circle ['sɜːkl] Kreis
cloak [kləʊk] Umhang
closely ['kləʊsli] genau
(to) **control** [kən'trəʊl] beherrschen
(to) **cough** [kɒf] husten; spucken
crash [kræʃ] **1** *Nomen* Krachen **2** *Verb* (to) **crash** krachen
crest [krest] Wappen
criminal ['krɪmɪnl] Verbrecher
cruel ['kruːəl] grausam
(to) **cut down** niederstrecken, töten

D

deep [diːp] tief
deer [dɪə] Reh, Hirsch
disguise [dɪs'gaɪz]: **in disguise** verkleidet

E

Earl [ɜːl] Graf
edge [edʒ] Rand
enemy ['enəmi] Feind
escape [ɪ'skeɪp] **1** *Nomen* Flucht
2 *Verb* (to) **escape** flüchten
everybody else alle anderen
evil ['iːvl] **1** *Adj* böse
2 *Nomen* **the evil** das Böse
(to) **expect** [ɪk'spekt] erwarten

F

(to) **face** [feɪs] gegenüberstehen
fame [feɪm] Ruhm
(to) **fear** [fɪə] sich fürchten
feast [fiːst] Festmahl
fiancée [fi'ɒnseɪ] Verlobte
fierce [fɪəs] heftig
fight [faɪt] Kampf
fighter ['faɪtə] Kämpfer
flour ['flaʊə] Mehl
foot: on foot zu Fuß
for now zur Zeit, jetzt
(to) **force** ['fɔːs] zwingen
forester ['fɒrɪstə] Waldbewohner
furious ['fjʊəriəs] wütend

G

(to) **gasp** [gɑːsp] tief einatmen; nach Luft schnappen
get out! verschwinde!
(to) **get worried** sich Sorgen machen
gold [gəʊld] Gold
(to) **grab** [græb] sich schnappen, packen
grandson ['grændsʌn] Enkel
greedy ['griːdi] gierig
grim [grɪm] grimmig
(to) **grin** [grɪn] grinsen
guard [gɑːd] **1** *Nomen* Wachposten
2 *Verb* (to) **guard** schützen
(to) **guess** vermuten

H

half halb, halbwegs
hall [hɔːl] Saal
(to) **hang** [hæŋ] (auf)hängen
hangman ['hæŋmæn] Henker
happily gern
harsh [hɑːʃ] schroff
heart [hɑːt] Herz
heavily ['hevɪli] **1** hoch
2 bedrückt
hen house ['hen] Hühnerstall
(to) **hiss** [hɪs] zischen
(to) **hold out** ausstrecken
Holy Land ['həʊli] das Heilige Land
honest ['ɒnɪst] ehrlich
hood [hʊd] Kapuze
horn [hɔːn] Horn
(to) **horrify** ['hɒrɪfaɪ] entsetzen
huge [hjuːdʒ] riesig
hut [hʌt] Hütte

I

idiot ['ɪdiət] Idiot
interest ['ɪntrəst] Zinsen

J

(to) **join** [dʒɔɪn] **1** sich anschließen
2 teilnehmen
(to) **joke** Witze machen

K

knelt [nelt]**:** (to) **kneel** [niːl] knien
knight [naɪt] Ritter

L
Lady *Adelstitel*
law [lɔː] Gesetz
leader ['liːdə] (An-)Führer
leaf [liːf] Blatt
leapt up [lept]**:** (to) **leap up** [liːp] hochspringen
look around sich umsehen
lord [lɔːd] *Adelstitel*
low [ləʊ] niedrig; tief

M
master ['mɑːstə] Herr
Midsummer's Day Sommersonnenwende
mill [mɪl] Mühle
miller ['mɪlə] Müller
(to) **mind** [maɪnd]**: you don't mind** es macht Ihnen nichts aus
monk [mʌŋk] Mönch

N
neck [nek] Hals
no longer nicht mehr
nobody else sonst niemand
(to) **nod** [nɒd] nicken
Norman ['nɔːmən]
1 Normanne
2 normannisch
nowhere ['nəʊweə] nirgendwohin

O
on foot zu Fuß
one by one einzeln
outdoor men ['aʊtdɔː] sportliche Männer
outlaw ['aʊtlɔː] Bandit
outside [ˌaʊt'saɪd] Außen-

P
platform Hinrichtungsplatz
poor: the poor die Armen
possible ['pɒsəbl] möglich
Prince [prɪns] Prinz
Prior ['praɪə] Prior, Klostervorsteher
prisoner ['prɪznə] Gefangener
probably ['prɒbəbli] wahrscheinlich
promise ['prɒmɪs] Versprechen
(to) **pull away** wegziehen
(to) **punish** ['pʌnɪʃ] bestrafen

R
(to) **raise** [reɪz] hochheben
ransom (money) ['rænsəm] Lösegeld
(to) **reach for** greifen nach
(to) **realise** ['rɪəlaɪz] erkennen
rent [rent] Miete, Pacht
(to) **reply** [rɪ'plaɪ] antworten
rescue Rettung
revenge [rɪ'vendʒ] Rache
rich: the rich die Reichen
right-hand man rechte Hand
rose [rəʊz]**:** (to) **rise** [raɪz] aufsteigen
ruler ['ruːlə] Herrscher
rusty ['rʌsti] rostig

S
Saxon ['sæksən] Sachse
scar [skɑː] Narbe
scroll [skrəʊl] Schriftrolle
servant ['sɜːvənt] Diener
shilling ['ʃɪlɪŋ] Shilling *(veraltete britische Währung)*
shocked ['ʃɔkd] schockiert

shout Ruf, Schrei
sick [sɪk]: **the sick** die Kranken
silently ['saɪləntli] still, ruhig
silver ['sɪlvə] Silber
simple-minded [ˌsɪmpl'maɪndɪd] einfältig
since [sɪns] weil
Sir mein Herr
(to) **slip** [slɪp] (aus)rutschen
so long ago vor langer Zeit
soldier ['səʊldʒə] Soldat
son-in-law ['sʌnɪnˌlɔː] Schwiegersohn
soot [sʊt] Ruß
sort of thing: that sort of thing so etwas
spy [spaɪ] Spion
St (= Saint) [snt] St (=Sankt)
staff [stɑːf] Stock
(to) **stare** [steə] starren
stick [stɪk] Stock
stood up [stʊd]: **stand up** [stænd] aufstehen
stop it! hör auf!
strong-looking kräftig aussehend
(to) **suffer** ['sʌfə] leiden
suit of armour [ˌsuːt əv 'ɑːmə] Ritterausrüstung
sword [sɔːd] Schwert
swung (at) [swʌŋ]: (to) **swing (at)** [swɪŋ] schwingen (gegen)

T

(to) **taste** [teɪst] probieren, kosten
Thank God Gott sei Dank
throne [θrəʊn] Thron
(to) **throw off: they had to throw themselves off the road** sie wurden von der Strasse gedrängt
to um zu;
To the king's safe return! Auf die sichere Rückkehr des Königs!
track [træk] Weg, Pfad
traitor ['treɪtə] Verräter
trap [træp] Falle
traveller ['trævələ] Reisender
turn: it was the giant's turn der Riese war an der Reihe; **it was the turn of Sir Guy** Sir Guy war an der Reihe
(to) **turn: turn away** sich abwenden; **turn back** zurückgehen

U

unconscious [ʌn'kɒnʃəs] bewusstlos

W

war [wɔː] Krieg
(to) **wave** [weɪv] winken (mit), schwenken, herumfuchteln
way of life Lebensweise
weak [wiːk] schwach
weapon ['wepən] Waffe
wedding ['wedɪŋ] Hochzeit
wedding service Trauungszeremonie
woods [wʊdz] Wald
wrestling competition ['reslɪŋ] Ringkampf
wrong [rɒŋ]:
There was something wrong. Etwas stimmte nicht.
This is very wrong. Dies ist großes Unrecht.

LIST OF NAMES AND PLACES

Barnsdale ['bɑːnzdeɪl]

Edward ['edwəd]

Fountains Abbey ['faʊntənz 'æbi]

Guy of Gisborne [gaɪ əv 'gɪzbɔːn]

Harold ['hærəld]
Huntingdon ['hʌntɪŋdən]

John ['dʒɒn]

Lee Castle [li 'kɑːsl]

Marian Fitzwalter ['mæriən 'fɪtzwɔːltə]
Much the Miller [mʌtʃ ðə 'mɪlə]

Nottingham ['nɒtɪŋhəm]

Patrick Fitzwalter ['pætrɪk 'fɪtzwɔːltə]

Richard of Lee ['rɪtʃəd əv li]
Robert Locksley ['rɒbət 'lɒksli]
Robin Hood ['rɒbɪn hʊd]

Sherwood ['ʃɜːwʊd]
St Mary's Abbey [snt 'meəriz 'æbi]

Westminster Abbey [westmɪnstə 'æbi]
Will Scarlet [wɪl 'skɑːlət]
William Scathlope ['wɪljəm 'skaθləʊp]
Wirral ['wɪrəl]
Worman ['wɔːmən]

Yorkshire ['jɔːkʃə]